Around & About

Hope Cove

and

Thurlestone

GW00673374

We all have our favourite places and the area 'around and about Hope Cove and Thurlestone' is most definitely one of mine. It has given me some wonderful walks and days out. This then is a small book for those who agree with me and want to 'take home' a little bit of the flavour of their visit, a reminder of those sunny days spent in one of the most beautiful parts of an extremely lovely county.

Here are some extracts, to set the scene, from a most unlikely source. Miss Marianne Farningham wrote this to the *Christian World* about a century ago. I am sure she never would have imagined that one day, so far into the future, she would be providing an introduction to this book!

"There are two delightful places in South Devon, beloved of artists, which are called Hope Cove and Thurlestone. The map of Devon reveals several considerable spaces as yet untouched by the railway; and among them is that which forms the extreme South of the country, and includes the land that lies above Prawle Point, from Start Bay on the East to Bigbury Bay on the West. Those who wish to be 'Far from the maddening crowd', and hold communion with Nature … may obtain here a Paradise of rest and pure pleasure. There are, indeed, plenty of villages to select from, but Hope is one of the best. Is it not a pretty name? There are seventeen or eighteen places in the British Isles that bear the same name; but surely the Hope of Devonshire is the loveliest of them

all ... The climate is delightful, such as may be enjoyed in the South of France, on the shores of the sunny Mediterranean ... The village is small, but extremely picturesque. Most of the houses are thatched, and a little artistic taste has been employed even in the thatching, so that they have a difference from that of the same class of cottages in the inland towns of the midland counties. There is a small inn, which is usually occupied by artists, for almost every year at the Academy are pictures which have been painted at Hope ... Also there are men and women of strong and striking individuality, whose faces are worth painting, and whose conversations are worth listening to. These people have lived by the sea, their bread is on the waters, the waves and wind have spoken to them, and in their brown faces and flashing eyes there are the marks of intercourse with Nature. They reverence the sea, and even fear it more than strangers do, because they know

its power. They have been robbed of their comrades in the great depths of the ocean; women have lost their husbands, and fathers, sons and brothers...

Even on a lovely summer's day there is a fresh breeze blowing, and the leaping waves are glorious sights to see. There is a magnificent walk over the downs to Thurlestone Sands, and the larks sing, and the wild flowers blossom, and the sea is so beautiful that such a walk will be long remembered...

An ideal summer holiday might be spent either at Thurlestone, or Inner or Outer Hope."

Let's see if things have changed since Marianne's time and perhaps discover some more of the history and heritage of this lovely stretch of coast for ourselves.

Thurlestone, located on rolling hills about a quarter of a mile from the sea, is a lovely village of quaint thatched cottages, many of them garlanded with roses, fuchsias and woodbine. Its popularity with holidaymakers has prevented a population decline so common in other parts and villages of the South Hams. There has been much new building and some say 'a little too much'!

The village takes its names from the distinctive Thurlestone Rock, which stands stoutly and

stubbornly resisting the might of the sea whilst all around it has been worn down to a slippery wave-cut platform of rocks and rock-pools. It was formed when the softer clay-slatey rocks surrounding it were worn away, leaving it isolated. This resistance has led to some homespun wisdom as we are told to "Brave every shock, Like Thurlestone's Rock". A guide book, written and researched about a century ago, about 'Salcombe and District' by James Fairweather had this to say of it: *"Lying just off the eastern end of these Sands is an arched rock of red Triassic conglomerate, resting upon Devonian clay slates. It is the most remarkable and peculiar rock on the south coast, and stands about thirty feet high, whilst it is forty feet long. The hole is twenty feet in height by ten broad. It can be approached at low water spring tides, and in a storm a peculiar noise, heard at a great distance, is caused by the rush of water through this hole, and is generally considered as an indication of approaching rain."*

It's fortunate that the voluntary artillery, who camped on 'Malborough Down' in 1803, didn't have any more ample firepower than was placed at their disposal; Thurlestone Rock was the object of their attention and from their lofty position they took pot shots at this famed sea-stack. Fortunately no discernible damage was done to it, so it must be as tough and resistant as people say it is!

'Thurlestone' means the holed or pierced stone. It is reputed that the awesome noise of the waves passing through it can sometimes be heard in Kingsbridge, about five miles away. Evidence has been found that there was once a forest below the low water mark but a steady rise in sea level, since the ice age, has drowned it to form the feature known as a 'submerged forest'.

The philosophical Harper, who wrote a guide book to the South Devon coastline in 1907, did so with great style and refreshing honesty. *"When the south-westerly winds bring great seas raging into the bay, with towering white combers dashing in upon the sands, the Thurlestone finds a voice and calls with a sound of roaring all over this countryside. The rustics say that at such times you shall hear the bellowing of the Thurlestone ten miles distant.*

For myself, I have come to Thurlestone at a time when there are no voices, save the catlike screaming of the gulls and the horrible squawking noises of the cruiser setting out from Hope Cove, and bidding a series of half-suffocated goodbyes with her steam whistles, dreadfully like some one being offensively sick. Noises are not common on Thurlestone strand, and I would even say it was lonely, save the millions of sand fleas inhabiting the shore, forbid the thought.

I have bought a piece of Dutch cheese and some biscuits, disregarding the inmates of the one hideously plastered boarding house recently built here, I take off my shoes and stockings, and sitting on a comfortable rock … make these notes. Two pennyworth of Dutch cheese, with biscuits to match, a comfortable seat on a rocky ledge, your feet dabbling in the clear water, and sunshine over all, will bring you into close relation with the Infinite…

There are cornelians and lovely pebbles on this lovely strand, and sea anemones, to the eye appetisingly like fruit-jellies, on the rocks. Alas! They are not good to eat, and as fairy gold, we all know, turns to sere leaves, so the translucent pebbles of the wet seashore become the commonplace opaque stones that the next day we turn disgustedly out of our pockets…"

These sands have witnessed some tragedies and it is not just the cries of Thurlestone Rock which have been borne on the wind! Fairweather added this chilling tale in an age when guide books didn't try to make everything look wonderful: *"It was here, about the year 1772, that the wreck of* Chantiloupe *occurred, a vessel returning from the West Indies. Those were the days when wrecking was practised in all its worst excess, and tortured with the fear of being murdered, a wealthy lady of the name of Burke put on her richest dresses, and awaited the final shock with her necklaces about her bosom, and her hands covered with jewellery. It is supposed she was related to the famous Edmund Burke, for as soon as the wreck of the vessel was known in London, he came down and stayed in the neighbourhood, stating that a relative of his was, he feared, on board. Most probably he never learnt what her fate was. By a strange coincidence, with the exception of one man, she was the only person thrown on shore alive, but so far from being protected by her magnificence, it attracted to her all the wreckers, who fought with one another as they tore the jewels from her neck, and cut off her swollen fingers to secure the rings upon them. Her body was buried in the sand but was dug up by a dog, when blood was discovered upon the ears and mutilated hands. A lady in the neighbourhood sent and had the body decently interred. The murderers could not be traced, but tradition says, that 'all the men in it came to a bad end'."*

Other accounts say the *Chantiloupe* ran aground in October 1757.

Over the years thousands of visitors have enjoyed trouble-free visits to these shores and the beaches of Thurlestone have attracted some famous visitors. Before Angela Rippon became known nationally she worked for a local newspaper and if there were a few hours of warm sunshine left in the day would make for Thurlestone. She wrote in her book *Angela Rippon's West Country* (1982): *"I've lain on that beach, scorched by the sun of July and August, watching the sails of small craft bob crimson and white against the sea, and echoed the thoughts of so many of my countrymen 'if only we could guarantee the weather, who would ever want to go abroad for their holidays'."*

Overlooking these lovely shores is the grey-stone Church of All Saints at Thurlestone, a distinctive building of local slate. During the English Civil War its rector, John Snell, was heavily involved in the action. He was chaplain to Charles I and stayed with the Royalist garrison in the besieged Salcombe Castle. At the end of the conflict articles of surrender were drawn up and one of the conditions was that he should be allowed to continue his living as Rector of Thurlestone. But some of the unforgiving locals, fervent Puritans, decided to get their revenge on him by taking all his worldly goods and twice stealing his farm stock. John Snell 'took the hint' and, with his wife, fled from the parish. However he obviously liked Thurlestone, because many years later, at the Restoration, he came back to spend his last few years here. His wife was buried in Exeter Cathedral and on her grave it tells us that she 'always accompanied her husband in his immense dangers with an intrepid mind'. One of his sons was Mayor of Exeter and another Archdeacon of Totnes.

The church, one way or another, has played a big part in the history of this village. Its history and heritage were encapsulated in a newspaper article which appeared on 29 April 1904. Here are some extracts from it: *"Yesterday was a great day for Thurlestone, when the historic parish church was rededicated by the Bishop of Exeter. The church was built in the thirteenth century, probably on the site of a still older church, for it has a fine Norman font of red sandstone ... In 1328 the church, which had been closed for a time on account of being polluted by bloodshed, was reopened by the Abbot of Buckfast, acting for the Archdeacon of Totnes, but it had to be closed again for three months because the parishioners would not pay their share of the fees for the service...*

The Church Restoration Fund was started by the Rev Hon R. J. Yarde-Buller, the brother of the patron, Lord Churston, and carried on by the present rector and the Restoration Committee...

The parish is a poor one, and the education authorities are pressing for a new Church school to be begun by next Spring ... The villagers showed their interest in the proceedings by a liberal display of flags and bunting ... The Bishop, the clergy, and the choir robed in the temporary church, and as they walked in procession, preceded by a cross-bearer, up the steep winding path

4   Hope Cove and Thurlestone

to the church singing 'Onward Christian Soldiers', the scene was most impressive. The church overlooks Bigbury Bay, and the St George's flag flying from the venerable tower, which has witnessed countless storms and westerly gales, must have been seen many miles distant on sea and land. To the seafarer the church is one of the most prominent landmarks on the Devonshire coast. There was a crowded congregation, many standing in the porch throughout the service...

After the service, the Bishop and clergy returned in procession to the temporary church, where they disrobed. Luncheon was served in Thurlestone House Hotel, many ladies and gentleman from a wide district being present – The Rector announced that the collection amounted to nearly £50. (Applause). He thanked Mr and Mrs Grose for placing their house and servants entirely at their disposal free of cost, also those ladies who had furnished the provisions...

A reception by his lordship at the rectory followed, and at evensong the sermon was preached by the Rev Hon R. J. Yarde-Buller."

The restoration work was carried out by Mr George Fellowes Prynne, the son of the apparently famous Vicar of St Peter's in Plymouth. The rector at the time was the Rev Frank Egerton Coope M.A. who wrote and published a marvellous book *Thurlestone Church and Parish*. He arrived at Thurlestone in 1897, Queen Victoria's 'Diamond Jubilee' year, and resigned the living in August 1921 to take up another in Sussex. It would be wonderful to go back in time and be taken on a tour of this lovely church by him, for he knew so much about it and was able to sprinkle secular anecdotes to add some spice to his description. Here are just a few, of the many, amusing or historic little stories included in his book:

"In ancient times the north door was set open when the devil was exorcised, as a broad hint to him to depart, but at the present time it is set open for the convenience of no-one more terrible than the sexton and the church-cleaner."

"There were some stocks which stood within the memory of man in the church porch, into which naughty boys were put who behaved badly in church. A drunken man, having been put in them once, afterwards carried them off and threw them into the stream at the bottom of Thurlestone Hill. They were brought back again, and, having been disused for many years, were built into a cottage as a lintel to a window by William Snowdon, who at ninety-two years of age could not remember which cottage it was."

"There used to be a Firepan, I am told, at one time supported by four oak posts upon the top of the turret of the tower, for lighting beacons upon. When I came here I was shown a statement in 'Black's Guide to Devon' that the first beacon-fire which announced that the Armada was in sight was lighted on Thurlestone Church tower."

"In the summer of 1898 a strong swarm of bees made their way from Thurlestone Hotel into the churchyard. Mr Grose, our excellent churchwarden, pursued them and tried to hive them with every blandishment that he could think of; but these bees were determined to do something for the church restoration fund, and promptly disappeared into a small hole in the side of the church tower. This hole led into a much larger one – about five feet long – which had formerly held a beam of the scaffold by means of which the tower was built. In the autumn of 1899 the Rector discovered that by moving one small stone it was possible to get at the honey. Mr Grose kindly came to the rescue and took it – not, perhaps, without some sad reflections upon the base way in which these bees had deserted him. With no small trouble to herself, Mrs Grose ran it out and prepared it for sale. It brought in twenty five shillings for the restoration fund."

"There was a pulpit of fourteenth century carved oak and some fine monuments in the east end, but the west end was all choked up with shaky wooden pillars. The choir sat in the gallery, and it used to creak and groan so loudly as they mounted to their places that we used to speculate how long it would be before it came down, and count up how many would be killed by its descent on their heads! However, the choristers were not alarmed at the prospect, though they were careful to put the fat farmer who played the big 'bass vile' in the strongest place in the centre, and the other instrumentalists – the violins and hautboys and flute – grouped around him."

And the Rev Frank Egerton Coope M.A. also included many more sombre observations which shed a light on what are now local landmarks. *"As I write steps are being taken to erect a granite village cross, copied from what I conceive to have been the original design of the ancient cross*

at South Zeal [near Okehampton]. *It will stand upon the village green outside the church yard to commemorate the men of the Parish who gave their lives for us during the Great War."*

An earlier nineteenth century rector did his best to promote and champion a teetotal environment. Mr Fox, in his guide book to the area, stated that: *"It is worthy to remark that in neither Thurlestone nor Buckland (as is the case with South Milton) can you find a single public house. The Rector has, so far, been successful in his determination to prevent the opening of any place for the sale of strong drink; knowing well its demoralising effect on the rural population."* Fortunately today you will discover that Thurlestone has the Village Inn, whose story as a family-run business is a fascinating one...

It must have been a colourful scene at Wadebridge railway station when, in 1895, Farmer William John Grose and his wife Margaret Amelia herded all their animals onto a special train to move to Devon's South Hams. If ever there was a case of literally moving 'lock, stock and barrel' then this was it. With every possession, and their four young sons, William, Howard, Cuthbert and James, they left North Cornwall bound for South Devon and a new life. But farming can be heartbreaking work and Mr Grose had the cruel misfortune to lose most of his livestock through disease. The landowner then terminated the Groses' lease, a deed that was destined to change the fate and function of the whole family and, ultimately, fashion their future.

The Grose family moved into a large farmhouse at Thurlestone. William and his wife had the foresight to see that the railway, which had brought them to the area, was also bringing large numbers of visitors, particularly golfers. This observation was duly noted on the first sign that they erected, which said, 'Thurlestone House, Golfers accommodated, Picnic parties catered for, Terms moderate'. It is likely that the initial success of their venture was down to Margaret Amelia's catering skills and the warm welcome which was given to all visitors. There was much repeat business as whole families returned, time after time, and the small hotel's reputation spread far and wide. One institution, which would be a novelty today, was that in those early days all the guests sat down to eat at one long table.

Margaret Amelia's cream teas were famed far and wide, even 'fit for a king' or someone approaching one. It seems that whilst the Prince of Wales (the future Edward VIII) was a cadet at the Royal Naval College at Dartmouth he and a number of friends visited Thurlestone for a round of golf. Afterwards they repaired to the hotel to enjoy one of these 'legendary' cream teas. It is rumoured that the young prince was 'crowned' in a mock ceremony here. Instead of a jewelled crown a waste paper bin, or possibly a chamber pot, was used by his friends. The building where this revelry took place is now the Village Inn.

Getting to the hotel, in its early days, was something of an adventure. Guests were conveyed from Kingsbridge Station, no longer in existence, by horse and carriage. William Grose acquired a fleet of conveyances which included broughams, wagonettes and Victorias. Guests who wanted to tour the outlying parts of the district could hire them. And as times moved on the foresight of the Groses ensured that they were the first in the area to have a fleet of cars, which included a Studebaker tourer, the envy of all for its ability to ascend the steep Aveton Gifford hill in top gear!

The intrepid Rev Egerton Coope described Thurlestone as a comparatively quiet place during the First World War: *"All our alarms arose from the sea; we heard and saw merchant vessels blown up and submarines captured or sunk, soldiers were quartered upon us, aeroplanes and airships patrolled the coast. A sharp, sometimes too sharp a lookout was kept for spies, and German submarine supplies were discovered hidden in sea caves. The church windows had to be shaded at night to prevent any light showing out to sea. The rings screwed into the wall-plates to support the curtains are still there."*

Inevitably the hotel grew after this conflict, in both reputation and size, with various building extensions added at regular intervals. This was essential so that the hotel could cope with the ever-increasing demand, and it entered something of a golden era and entertained many rich and famous guests. At one stage a unique claim could be made: every woman in Thurlestone either was employed, or had been employed at some time, in the hotel.

The Second World War greatly disrupted things and also took its toll on both the village and the hotel. Two girls' schools from Eastbourne initially commandeered the hotel in 1940. But their stay was short-lived because, in 1941, the Royal Marines requisitioned it as an official training depot. The Groses' personal home The Bungalow (they had moved to Kingsbridge) became a hospital and some of the Thurlestone

villagers were born there! In 1945 Margaret Amelia passed away, but what a legacy she left behind in her hotel.

The wartime damage to the hotel's structure and fabric was considerable. Expensive dining room curtains were requisitioned and taken to Devonport to be cut up for dusters; structural damage to the roof was caused because the leadings were not taken into consideration when a heavy anti-aircraft gun was sited there; a cherished polished floor was ruined and had to be renovated.

Following the war, petrol rationing continued until 1949. The isolated location of the hotel became a positive disadvantage and a worrying time followed. For a long while, until 1971, the hotel was more or less obliged to close each winter. Since then an improved road network, combined with an increase in personal wealth and leisure time, has enabled the Thurlestone Hotel to thrive once again. It is now a luxuriously appointed hotel, in a wonderful location. One unusual attraction is a fireplace, beautifully inlaid with rosewood and applewood, that was once owned by Richard Adams, author of *Watership Down*.

For those who walk up the main street of Thurlestone, it's worth looking at the two-faced pub sign for the Village Inn, for it tells a story of a Spanish vessel mentioned later in the Hope Cove part of the book.

Thurlestone has to possess one of the most beautifully situated golf courses in England, but it is hard to imagine what it was like just over a century ago, in 1897, when it was begun. At that time this was a derelict and fairly remote stretch of coastline of overgrown scrubland. Like so many places along this coast it was known as The Warren because a rabbit warren, not unlike Watership Down in some respects, existed on the fifty-acre site that had been earmarked for the intended golf course. Four men, T. W. Latham (surveyor/architect), H. G. Prowse (brewery owner), A. B. Crispin (retired auctioneer), and Dr E. A. S. Elliott (a

retired local doctor) were the pioneers of this first, rather crude course through an almost impenetrable jungle of vegetation. This quintessential quartet all had nicknames bestowed upon them. These were fine examples of alliteration for they were the AA to DD of the golf club's humble beginnings. Respectively, they were the Artful Architect, the Bow-windowed Brewer, the Courtly Count and the Drunken Doctor! The first President was Lord Mildmay, an important landowner in this area.

Once the prickly problem of injury-threatening vegetation had been solved the club was able to move on to better things. Forty-eight (35 men and 13 ladies) carefully selected members, who conducted themselves "at all times in a civilised fashion", pulled together to improve things slowly, but the first clubhouse was something of a letdown. It had no water supply and, initially, buckets of water had to be carried all the

way down from the village, about half a mile away! The club's 'elite' members still had to contend with strong winds, narrow fairways and a nineteenth hole which was a Spartan affair by today's standards. Playing a round of golf must have been like going on safari because there were sheep and cattle grazing on the course and hundreds of rabbits scampering about.

During the Second World War it was one of the few courses to remain open because there were many servicemen stationed here to protect the coastline from invasion and they needed to be kept amused and fit.

After the Second World War, when the beaches and scenery slowly began to attract visitors again, the course underwent a major transformation. Today it covers much the same area, an open, treeless, 'bracing' cliff-top course of soft springy turf along its 6,337 yards.

Harry Pratt achieved national fame in 1974 when, at the tender age of seven years, he became the youngest golfer to sink a 'hole-in-one' at the 111-yard sixth hole. But did he have to buy a round of drinks at the nineteenth hole?

There are a number of ways to get from Thurlestone to Bantham. There is the pleasant cliff-top jaunt along the seaward edge of the course to enjoy the sea-stacks and waves. There is also the shorter 'inland' route from Thurlestone Church along the top edge of the golf course. This rises gently to a fine vantage point before the land then seems to suddenly fall away to Bantham well below. This stunning view reveals that here there are golden sands and the fine Avon estuary. It also peers down onto the rooftops of the small village of Bantham, which has wisely taken a step back from the sea and all its fickle moods. Those with good eyesight might just pick out the neighbouring golf course on the heights beyond the Avon.

South Milton, slightly inland, is just a vowel away from matching the name of a North Devon market town. It is a small village whose population has remained fairly constant for many years. Since 1851 it has hovered around the 400 mark, although in 1901 it dipped to a low of 287, but now the village is growing again slowly and steadily. Once more the church of All Saints is the most obvious landmark of a community which has developed near the head of a short stream which flows into the sea at 'Thurlestone Sands', about a mile away to the south-west. Early in the twentieth century it underwent a major restoration programme, the fourth in the district in the care of the Ven Archdeacon Earle. He had supervised the restoration of West Alvington and Malborough and had been the overseer for the new church at Galmpton which replaced the ruined church at nearby South Huish, in the next valley again. Here are just a few lines from a dull report. *"The fine old church of South Milton ... was reopened yesterday by the Lord Bishop of Exeter ...*

The pulpit, which is entirely new, is of oak on a stone base, and is of excellent proportions. A very hand-some brass lectern has been sup-plied by Messrs Whippell [sic] of Exeter, and placed in position ... An organ of fourteen stops has been placed in the north chapel, and is the gift of Mr Maclellan, of Horswell House ... The church has been fitted with a heating appara-tus in lieu of the stoves used hith-erto. The whole of the work has been carried out in a conscientious and substantial manner, and to the satisfaction of all concerned ... There was a public tea in the afternoon, which was numerously attended, and in the evening the Ven Archdeacon of Totnes was announced to preach."

There are certain names which seem to predominate in this churchyard, the Lidstones, Luscombes and Steers being just some of the families which spanned many generations. Also buried in this quiet place is poor Hubert Baker who was murdered in the summer of 1904. A full account of his fate is in another of my books *Along the Avon or Aune.*

South Milton's Village Hall was used in the filming of *Supergrass,* a feature film made by the 'Comic Strip' team. The film starred many actors with a strong Devon connection and included Dawn French, Jennifer Saunders, Adrian Edmondson, Robbie Coltrane, Nigel Planer, Peter Richardson, Alexei Sayle, Keith Allen, Michael Elphick and the late Ronald Allen who, for many years, played the part of David Hunter in the early television soap about a motel in the Midlands, *Crossroads.*

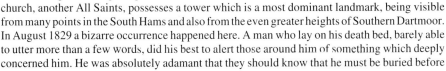

South Huish has a ruined church, in the quietest of rural backwaters surrounded by an agricultural community, where farmers and families, for many centuries, worshipped. This small thirteenth century church, built of cragstone, was the scene of a drama in 1867 when a window was blown in during Divine Service and almost killed the priest. It was 'the last straw' – although it was situated in 'a deep vale of romantic beauty', it was abandoned and allowed to become an overgrown ruin. The Earl of Devon provided land for a new church at Galmpton, which was better located for many of the flock.

As is the way of things, a lot of interest and enthusiasm was generated and ways of saving the ruin of St Andrew were considered. The saviours came in the shape of 'The Friends of Friendless Churches' who have effected many structural repairs and rendered it safe. Many visitors like to make their way along the quiet lanes to try to find it.

Malborough is the highest place featured in this book and its church, another All Saints, possesses a tower which is a most dominant landmark, being visible from many points in the South Hams and also from the even greater heights of Southern Dartmoor. In August 1829 a bizarre occurrence happened here. A man who lay on his death bed, barely able to utter more than a few words, did his best to alert those around him of something which deeply concerned him. He was absolutely adamant that they should know that he must be buried before

midday on the day of his imminent funeral. To this end he told them that they must heed his hard-spoken words. He passed away the next day, his family made his funeral arrangements, and the day of the funeral duly arrived. Whether there was a delay or whether they had chosen to ignore his words, I do not know, but he was not in his grave before noon. Exactly on the stroke of midday, a terrific thunderclap sounded, accompanied by a terrifying thunderbolt which shook the very fabric of the church. Fearing a disaster like the one which befell Widecombe when four people were killed and thirty maimed, the congregation made their exit – hard on the heels of the vicar who led the charge! Left behind, and all alone, in the church was the deceased. Maybe he had somehow known that there would be trouble and he wanted to be well out of the way … or maybe it was his way of expressing his displeasure at their failure to fulfil his last request. In any event, it was quite a time before the storm subsided and even longer before the coffin could be buried, because of the water-filled grave.

The graveyard contains some unusual and interesting epitaphs belonging to the victims of shipwrecks in nearby Bigbury Bay. Before Salcombe got its own parish church all the dead were brought up the very long hill for burial at Malborough. If you have ever walked or cycled from the water's edge at Salcombe to the church at Malborough, then you will appreciate what a tiring journey it was.

It is likely that Malborough, which means 'Maerla's fortified hill', was more important in the past than it is today, because it had many more shops and more tradesmen.

The village is divided into two parts, Higher Town and, yes, you have guessed, Lower Town, and I am sure you can also work out why. Who needs guide books? The village primary school draws from a wide catchment, is near the church and wedged between Higher Town and Lower Town.

For some people, Malborough has been a place of inspiration. Irene Roberts, who married the talented artist Trevor Roberts, moved to Devon from London, in the late 1960s. To date she has written a staggering 128 novels, under various names and for a number of leading publishers.

In recent years Malborough has played host to some lively folk festivals with participants drawn from far afield. The Royal Oak is the centre of attraction for the village's folk music scene, with mirth, merriment and music much in evidence at regular get-togethers there.

The way back to the coast and, literally, our last port of call is along high-hedged lanes. The cycle ride from Malborough down to Hope is the sort with which I can usually cope, and so we reach the sea again.

Hope Cove, also referred to in the past as 'Bolt Stay', is over the cliffs from Thurlestone and cosily tucked away in the corner of Bigbury Bay, lying, almost snugly, behind its breakwater and beneath the heights of Bolt Tail. In recent years the village has more than doubled its population despite a decline in its fishing industry, once its mainstay.

Mr Fox, of Kingsbridge, penned this lovely description of Hope Cove in 1874: *"This usually quiet little cove sometimes presents a curious spectacle, from its being a sheltered retreat for wind-bound vessels, which occasionally lie there for a week, or more, at least, until the breeze is a favourable one. We have seen between fifty and sixty vessels lying at anchor, at the same time, within a limited space; and then the villages presented a very animated scene, from the influx of sailors, both foreign and English, who came ashore, and caused great demand for provisions of various kinds. Cart after cart arrived with butchers' meat and loaves of bread, and were as*

speedily emptied of their loads, with much laughter and vociferation. Then came the filling of water casks from the clean spring just in front of one of the inns; and the discovery of water-cresses in an adjoining meadow. How they raced and chased, and vaulted over the stone hedge, and then came back again with caps, and handkerchiefs, and arms full of this wholesome and pleasant vegetable."

At that time there were only about a hundred villagers and with land transport extremely limited, in its range and variety, most goods came by sea. Hope Cove was also reliant upon hauliers and visiting traders for its daily needs. Locals rarely ventured far and news was often slow to reach this once remote place. Visitors coming here from large centres of population must have felt that they had stepped back in time. However, many were glad of this stark contrast and really could 'get away from it all'.

James Fairweather, of Salcombe, was another writer who saw the place a century ago: *"Leaving Galmpton the road gradually descends for about a mile to the village of Outer Hope, which is only separated from Inner Hope by a short road that rapidly ascends and then just as rapidly descends ... There is a small Inn, the Hope and Anchor, and several lodging houses ... In recent years several neat and pretty villas have been erected near the coast, and Hope is slowly developing as a visiting resort. The Shippens, the lookout of the coastguards, is a commanding and important eminence, and from here may be obtained the most extensive view of the surrounding coast and neighbourhood. Close to the flagstaff is an old cannon recovered from the wreck of the* Ramillies. *There is a beach, which is nicely sheltered ... During certain winds vessels put in here for shelter, but never probably so many at one time as on the 3rd day of September, 1855, when there were nearly sixty vessels of various sizes anchored within a short distance of each other, and these usually quiet villages, by the influx of so many sailors, became a scene of great bustle and animation."*

One time that Hope Cove did not appear a good place to be was during the cold winter of 1947 when blizzards cut off the village. Fortunately for the locals, they were not deprived of food and medical essentials as these were brought around the coast by the Salcombe Lifeboat *Samuel and Marie,* which even brought a doctor!

Hope Cove is a small resort but many people visit it, mostly by car, as is seen in the lanes leading to it. The number of 'passing places' has increased in recent years and the state of the hedgerows, through the volume of traffic, shows that it's not the quiet backwater it used to be. However, it's still a very beautiful place and well worth the inevitable reversing to get there. It was certainly appreciated by the film makers who made *Supergrass,* mentioned earlier, as they used Hope Cove for much of the filming. In one memorable scene, Robbie Coltrane, who is something of a 'man-mountain', unflinchingly walked along the breakwater whilst quite large waves broke over him.

Having myself walked along the top of this construction on a calm day, and found it decidedly slippery, makes Mr Coltrane's performance seem quite remarkable! What was unusual about this film is that in normal circumstances fictitious names are used; but 'Hope Cove' enjoyed the free publicity which it was given.

The biggest place of accommodation at Hope Cove is the Cottage Hotel, the largest single employer, which sits on an elevated spot between the two parts of the village. It has grown considerably since the time when it was called 'Westerly'. During the Second World War, the hotel was home to the aircrew flying from RAF Bolt Head airfield. According to a 1950s guide to Kingsbridge, there is "a miniature cabin made entirely of material obtained from the *Herzogin Cecilie*". Different owners have added and altered earlier structures, and although there were local protests, at different times, the hotel has evolved into a fine place to stay.

The Square at Inner Hope is admired by those who stumble across it. It is formed of thatched houses, some of which reflect the mood or appeal of the place; Devonia with its weather vane of

a sailing ship; Rambler Cottage, a reminder of the wonderful walks in the district; Mariner Cottage for those who have salt water coursing through their veins; Driftwood for the ancient salt-stained timbers washed ashore; and Croak's Pad, perhaps the ultimate retreat from the rat-race of the 'outside world'.

But Hope Cove is a place essentially to do with the sea, the village's larder, which has dominated its history, shaped its destiny and been its livelihood since time immemorial. The nature of the sea bed just offshore, and the quality of water, meant that crabs and lobsters, some of monstrous proportions, could be caught in great numbers. Before the First World War these were kept alive in storage pots in the calm water beneath Bolt Tail until an inter-coastal vessel came to collect them. Once aboard they were stored in the sloop's well to keep them alive and 'fresh' until getting to market. Following the First World War the crab and lobster haul was transported by rail from Kingsbridge, but the closing of the line and improvements in the motorway system mean that now they are transported by road to London, most ending up eventually in Spain (where the British go to end up looking like lobsters!).

The crab-pots were made locally even though the fishermen of Hope Cove didn't have the advantage of their own reed bed like their counterparts at Hallsands and Beesands in Start Bay. They relied on local farmers who possessed withy groves. An examination of an Ordnance Survey map shows that the valleys of the streams leading into Bigbury Bay often had marshy meadows ideal for the growing of withies. Eventually reeds from distant parts replaced locally-grown withies, but these were, in turn, replaced by pots made of synthetic materials.

The seasonal pilchard industry was also important, particularly in the mid-nineteenth century, until the main shoals diminished. A fuller account of this industry can be read in a sister book to this one, *Around & About Burgh Island and Bigbury-on-Sea*.

Bigbury Bay is a perilous place in times of storm and tempest so it's not surprising to discover that there is a former lifeboat house at Inner Hope. It was established in 1878 by the Grand Lodge of Freemasons as a thank-you offering for the recovery of the Prince of Wales, who had experienced a serious illness the previous year. His emblem, the 'Plume of Feathers', can be seen on the front wall. The name of the first lifeboat was *Alexandra* (the Princess of Wales), and its three successors continued this royal trend.

If a vessel was shipwrecked along this coast, it was almost certain that any attempts to rescue its crew would be hazardous in the extreme. Not many ships went aground in calm weather! There are several recorded instances of brave deeds by the local lifeboatmen in their valiant attempts to save lives. Between 1878 and 1930, many people were rescued by the various Hope Cove crews. When the *Jebba* ran ashore at Bolt Tail, two lifeboatmen, Isaac Jarvis and Jack Argeat, somehow bravely managed to scale the almost sheer, 200 feet high cliff in pitch darkness in order to carry the equipment to rig up a bosun's chair back to sea level. They thus saved 117 passengers, whilst the rest of the crew rescued the remaining 38 people. For their amazing deeds the two men received the Albert Medal (now the George Cross).

In its 52-year life span the Hope Cove lifeboat witnessed many moments of high drama; but in 1930 a decision was made to close this lifeboat station because Salcombe's had reopened with a new and more up to date motor boat. The last *Alexandra* was moved to Cromer in Norfolk, where she became number two boat.

However, the dramatic rescues on this coastline continued. During the Second World War ex-coxswain Isaac Jarvis, member of a famous Hope Cove family, was out fishing with his grandson, Eric, in his motor vessel when an American 'Flying Fortress' ditched into the sea. Isaac, who was then 78 years old, did not hesitate but made towards the plane as quickly as he could. By the time he reached the crash point the aircrew had scrambled into their inflatable dinghy. With a rough sea it was essential to get them to shore. Despite the danger all the ten airmen were hauled onto the fishing boat and, vastly overloaded, they made it back to the safety of the shore.

Beyond Bolt Tail to the east, towards Salcombe, many vessels have foundered on the rocks beneath mountainous cliffs. The uninsured *Herzogin Cecilie* is perhaps the most famous victim, not because of the scale of the disaster but because of her great beauty. In April 1936 thousands

 of spectators came to see her lying stricken at Soar Mill Cove and tales are told of how farmers ex-tracted 'a king's ransom' from those who wanted to park as close as possible or even simply gain access to the cliffs above her. She was the winner of long-haul grain races. However, she had a chequered ca-reer and there were those who regarded her as an unlucky ship. In her last years she experienced many mishaps, losing sails, suffering an explosion which killed two of the crew and colliding with another vessel. When she met her fate she was Finnish-owned. Captain Sven Eriksson had a premonition that she would go aground and his wife had pleaded with him not to leave Falmouth. Unlike many other shipwrecks it did not occur in stormy conditions but in foggy weather, which was cited as part of the cause of her fate. The captain was mystified (no pun intended) to strike land where and when he did. There was talk of the ship's compass being affected by the strong iron content found in the cliffs between Bolt Head and Bolt Tail. Pictures of her, of which there must have been many thousands, now fetch a healthy price at postcard auctions. More details of her demise are included in *Around & About Salcombe*, a publication which includes a circular walk from Malborough through Hope Cove, over Bolt Tail, across Bolberry Down and back to the starting place. It gives a lot of background information on the places passed along the way.

Closer to Hope the great but menacing cliffs of Bolt Tail have witnessed some high drama. The headland's great heights provided a grandstand view of the Spanish Armada in 1588. On Saturday 20 May thousands of spectators gathered to witness the scene of a fleet of 140 Spanish galleons, in a crescent-like formation, sailing up the English Channel. Despite their superior size several of the Spanish ships were chased completely around the British Isles. These included one of the fleet's two hospital ships, *St Peter the Great (San Pedro)*. This unfortunate ship went aground on the Shippen at Hope Cove on 28 October 1588. Eight of the ship's officers were held in custody at nearby Ilton Castle, ten were sent to Kingsbridge, whilst the rest of the crew were imprisoned at the inn at Hope Cove.

Almost everything from its wreck was salvaged, which led to some interesting improvisations. 'The Cabin' at Hope Cove is supposedly built from the timbers of this ship, as are other buildings in the area.

Bolt Tail is a great rocky fortress, an awesome headland that has witnessed many tragedies. Of the numerous ships which have been driven against it, the biggest disaster was that of the 1700-ton wooden-walled HMS *Ramillies* (formerly the *Royal Katherine*) which, after being separated from the rest of the ships in her fleet, and despite a frantic battle with the elements, went aground on 15 February 1760.

It was believed that a combination of poor navigation and a lack of awareness of where she was led to her fate. Her captain believed that he was farther west, off the coast of Plymouth. Burgh Island was thus mistaken for Looe Island. Captain Taylor navigated to the east of this into what he thought was the safe anchorage of Plymouth Sound. However, one of his crew had recognised this sweep of coastline as that of Bigbury Bay and tried to tell him. Instead of listening to this well-intentioned interjection Captain Taylor had the man charged with insubordination and clapped in irons. By the time the error was realised the vessel was embayed. And so it was that the *Ramillies*, instead of sailing into the safe waters of Plymouth Sound, met her fate. The death toll was excessive: 708 people perished out of a total of 734 on board, and badly decomposed bodies were washed up all along the length of Bigbury Bay in the following weeks. For many years afterwards gruesome finds of skeletons were common in the bay. Most of the 26 survivors, of whom only one was an officer, escaped by scaling the near vertical cliffs, a most perilous escape route. The small inlet where she grounded is now Ramillies Cove.

If the weather is fine, or simply dry, one could easily spend a week, or more, exploring this coastline and the immediate inland countryside on foot. For those who like history there is much more to discover, because we have only skimmed the surface.